CRUSADES
THE STRUGGLE FOR
THE HOLY LANDS

A mounted knight charged into battle.

Crusaders stormed the walls of Jerusalem using a seige tower.

Crusaders attacked the fortified city walls.

A defensive formation of shields, known as a "tortoise".

12th-century Byzantine troops

CRUSADES
THE STRUGGLE FOR THE HOLY LANDS

A 14th-century
war sword

Written by
MELANIE AND CHRISTOPHER RICE
AND CHRISTOPHER GRAVETT

Illustrated by
PETER DENNIS

A Dorling Kindersley Book

Dorling **DK** Kindersley

LONDON, NEW YORK, SYDNEY, DELHI, PARIS,
MUNICH and JOHANNESBERG

Project Editor Emma Johnson
Art Editor/Visualizer James Marks
Senior Editor Scarlett O'Hara
Deputy Managing Art Editor Vicky Wharton
Managing Editor Sue Grabham
Senior Managing Art Editor Julia Harris
DTP Designer Andrew O'Brien
Picture Researcher Julia Harris-Voss
Jacket Designer Dean Price
Production Shivani Pandey and Jenny Jacoby

First published in 2001
by Dorling Kindersley Limited
80 Strand, London WC2R 0RL

2 4 6 8 10 9 7 5 3

A CIP catalogue record for this book is available
from the British Library.

ISBN 0 7513 5894 0

Reproduced by Colourscan, Singapore
Printed and bound by L.E.G.O., Italy

Additional illustrations by Ray Grinaway
and David Ashby

see our complete
catalogue at
www.dk.com

Contents

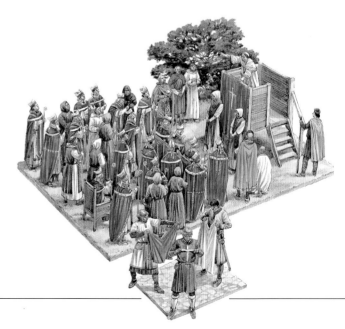

The Medieval World

A peasant cutting back vine branches.

A worker storing grain in a sack.

FOR HUNDREDS OF YEARS, MOST OF EUROPE HAD BEEN RULED BY THE Romans. Most Romans worshipped their own gods until AD 313, when Christianity became the offical religion. By the time of the First Crusade, in 1096, life for the people of medieval Europe was becoming stable, even prosperous. But religious conflict was about to unsettle this calm existence – the crusades were about to begin.

The Duc de Berry ordered this painting. It shows his castle and estate in France.

A labourer on the Duc de Berry's estate.

Symbol of faith
Christians believe that Jesus Christ is the Son of God. Christianity teaches that Jesus was crucified (died on a cross) so that those who have faith in him will go to heaven. The symbol of Christianity is a cross or crucifix (a cross with a figure of Jesus). This gold crucifix was made in England around the year AD 1000. The figure of Christ is carved in ivory.

Monks or nuns lived in an abbey.

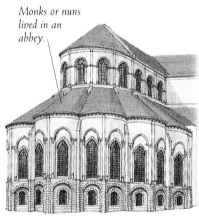

13th-century St Denis Abbey, France

Churches and mosques
A church or an abbey was at the centre of every Christian town and village. Likewise, every Muslim town had a mosque. The worship of God (or Allah to Muslims) was so important that every available builder and artist worked on the church or mosque.

ALMORAVIDS
The Moors called on the Muslim Almoravids of North Africa to help them in their struggle with the Christians in Spain. The Almoravids fought bravely, but the Christian crusaders were victorious.

A WORLD DIVIDED

BY ABOUT AD 300 THE ROMAN EMPIRE had become too vast to rule, so the emperor divided it into two. The east became the Byzantine Empire, with its capital at Constantinople. In the west, some countries began to govern themselves. The Byzantines and the people of western Europe were Christians. In AD 637 Arabs, who were Muslims, captured Jerusalem – a holy city for Muslims, Christians, and Jews. The Arabs allowed Christians to travel through their lands. When the warlike Seljuks took control of the region, however, it became dangerous for Christians. The later conflict between Muslims and Christians led to the crusades.

CHRISTIANS
There were Christians in the Roman world even before Christianity was officially tolerated by the Romans in AD 313. In Spain, Christians fought for hundreds of years to drive Arab settlers, called Moors, from southern Spain. In 1492, Granada was the last Moorish kingdom to fall.

ENGLAND

Christians

FRANCE

MEDITERRANEAN SEA

SPAIN

ALMORAVID EMPIRE

Cordoba
Granada

Almoravids

AFRICA

The sacred niche of the Great Mosque at Cordoba

CITY OF THE MOORS
The Moors had their splendid capital at Cordoba, which was described as the "jewel of the world" by 10th-century writers. The city had 700 mosques, including the lavishly decorated Great Mosque. It also had 70 libraries, 900 bathhouses, thousands of palaces, and the first street lights in Europe.

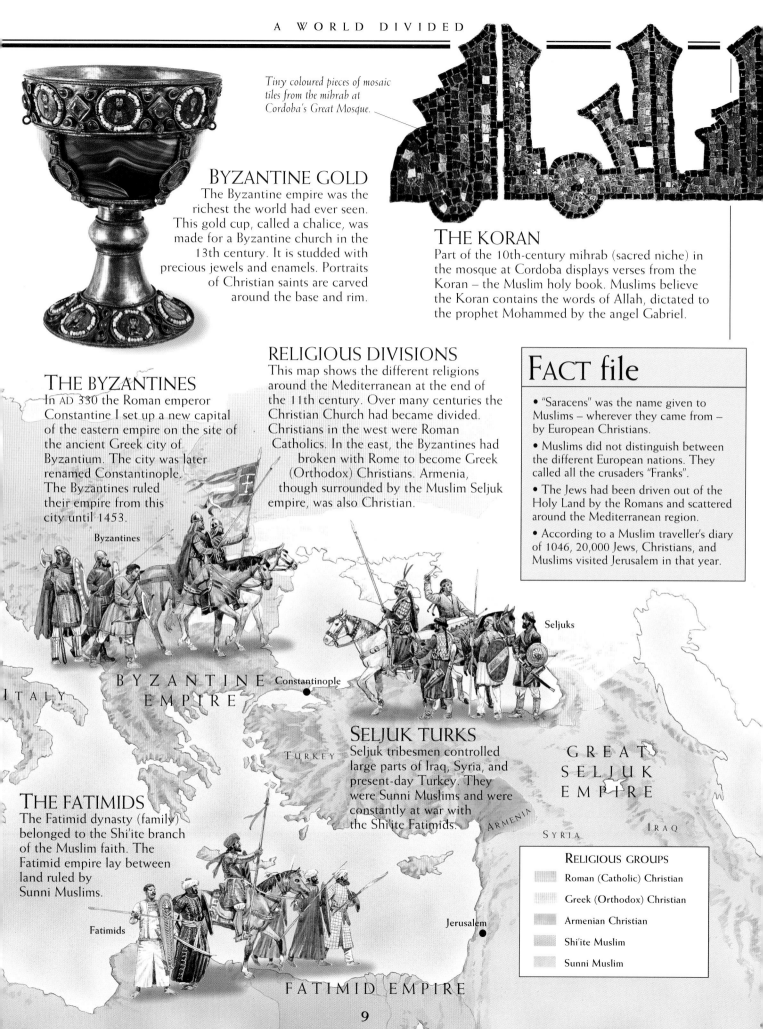

Tiny coloured pieces of mosaic tiles from the mihrab at Cordoba's Great Mosque.

BYZANTINE GOLD

The Byzantine empire was the richest the world had ever seen. This gold cup, called a chalice, was made for a Byzantine church in the 13th century. It is studded with precious jewels and enamels. Portraits of Christian saints are carved around the base and rim.

THE KORAN

Part of the 10th-century mihrab (sacred niche) in the mosque at Cordoba displays verses from the Koran – the Muslim holy book. Muslims believe the Koran contains the words of Allah, dictated to the prophet Mohammed by the angel Gabriel.

THE BYZANTINES

In AD 330 the Roman emperor Constantine I set up a new capital of the eastern empire on the site of the ancient Greek city of Byzantium. The city was later renamed Constantinople. The Byzantines ruled their empire from this city until 1453.

Byzantines

RELIGIOUS DIVISIONS

This map shows the different religions around the Mediterranean at the end of the 11th century. Over many centuries the Christian Church had became divided. Christians in the west were Roman Catholics. In the east, the Byzantines had broken with Rome to become Greek (Orthodox) Christians. Armenia, though surrounded by the Muslim Seljuk empire, was also Christian.

FACT file

• "Saracens" was the name given to Muslims – wherever they came from – by European Christians.

• Muslims did not distinguish between the different European nations. They called all the crusaders "Franks".

• The Jews had been driven out of the Holy Land by the Romans and scattered around the Mediterranean region.

• According to a Muslim traveller's diary of 1046, 20,000 Jews, Christians, and Muslims visited Jerusalem in that year.

ITALY

BYZANTINE EMPIRE   Constantinople

Seljuks

SELJUK TURKS

Seljuk tribesmen controlled large parts of Iraq, Syria, and present-day Turkey. They were Sunni Muslims and were constantly at war with the Shi'ite Fatimids.

TURKEY

GREAT SELJUK EMPIRE

ARMENIA

SYRIA   IRAQ

THE FATIMIDS

The Fatimid dynasty (family) belonged to the Shi'ite branch of the Muslim faith. The Fatimid empire lay between land ruled by Sunni Muslims.

Fatimids

Jerusalem

RELIGIOUS GROUPS

Roman (Catholic) Christian

Greek (Orthodox) Christian

Armenian Christian

Shi'ite Muslim

Sunni Muslim

FATIMID EMPIRE

THE JEWEL OF BYZANTIUM

CONSTANTINOPLE WAS THE GLITTERING capital of the Byzantine Empire. It was well defended on its southern side by the Sea of Marmara, and a narrow inlet formed a perfect harbour, the Golden Horn. The city stood on the Bosphorus, the channel leading to the Black Sea, it was also on the sea route from Russia to the Mediterranean, and camel caravan routes from Asia to eastern Europe. The markets were full of exotic spices and silks. Christian churches were bright with frescoes (wall paintings) and mosaics. In March 1095, the Byzantine Emperor Alexius II asked Pope Urban for help to fight the Seljuk Turks, who had invaded part of his empire and were close to Constantinople. On learning that the Byzantine (eastern) Christians were under threat from the Muslim Seljuks, Pope Urban was determined to help.

"NEW ROME"

Constantine called his city "New Rome", because it continued Roman achievements in building and town planning. Constantinople was a rich city with great palaces, Roman-style forums, and a cistern (underground water storage system).

Cistern

Forum of Arcadius

Forum Bovis

Land walls

Harbour of Eleutherion

BIGGEST CITY

Constantinople (right) grew into a huge city, rivalling ancient Rome in size and population. Greeks, Armenians, Russians, Italians, Jews, Bulgars, Khazars, and Turks lived among the riches of this great city. At the time of the crusades, Christians made up more than half of the city's population.

MIGHTY WALLS

The outer walls of Constantinople, built in about AD 420, were a great obstacle to invaders. Behind a 18-m (60-ft) wide moat, three walls rose in levels, each one overlooking the one in front. The towers were staggered so that every gap was filled with an archer or a catapult.

Two-handed axe

VARANGIAN GUARD

The Byzantine emperors had a bodyguard of Viking warriors – the Varangian guard – who had come to Constantinople through Russia. They were known for the two-handed axes they carried, and for their hard drinking.

FACT file

- There were 192 towers on the middle and inner walls around the city of Constantinople.
- There were 20 km (13 miles) of walls and 50 fortified gates enclosing the city, making it the strongest outpost of Christianity in the east.
- The Byzantine Empire was one of the most cultured and civilized of the time. In spite of this, 29 of its emperors met violent deaths.

MOSAIC MAGIC

Many Christian churches in Constantinople were decorated with mosaics – a technique of fixing thousands of tiny pieces of coloured glass and stone to a wall. This mosaic shows Christ with Emperor Constantine IX and the Empress Zoë, who ruled the Byzantine Empire from 980–1055.

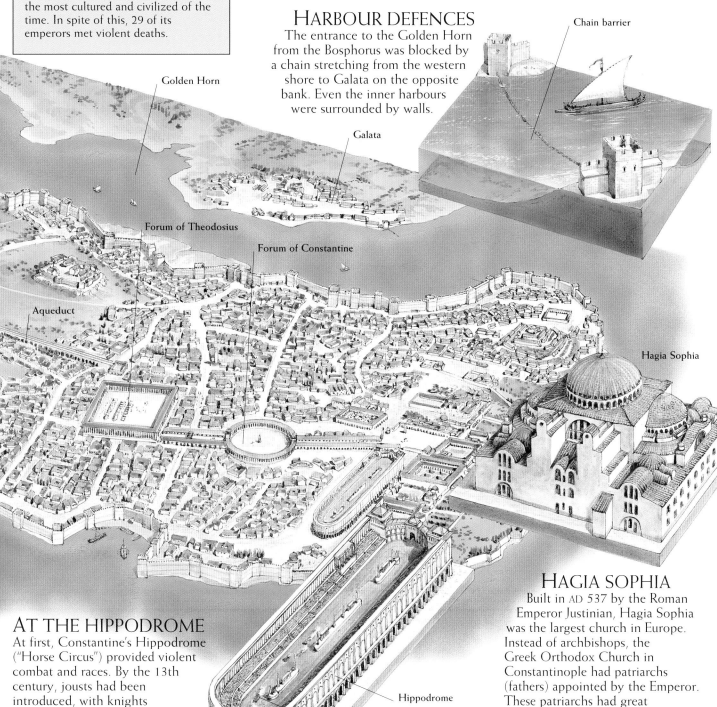

HARBOUR DEFENCES

The entrance to the Golden Horn from the Bosphorus was blocked by a chain stretching from the western shore to Galata on the opposite bank. Even the inner harbours were surrounded by walls.

Chain barrier

Golden Horn

Galata

Forum of Theodosius

Forum of Constantine

Aqueduct

Hagia Sophia

AT THE HIPPODROME

At first, Constantine's Hippodrome ("Horse Circus") provided violent combat and races. By the 13th century, jousts had been introduced, with knights fighting each other on horseback. Executions were also carried out here.

Hippodrome

Chariots racing

HAGIA SOPHIA

Built in AD 537 by the Roman Emperor Justinian, Hagia Sophia was the largest church in Europe. Instead of archbishops, the Greek Orthodox Church in Constantinople had patriarchs (fathers) appointed by the Emperor. These patriarchs had great influence. Missionaries from Hagia Sophia spread Byzantine culture into eastern Europe and Russia.

A PILGRIM'S JOURNEY

A pilgrim's seal, found in St John's basilica at Ephesus, Turkey.

A PILGRIM IS A PERSON WHO makes a special journey to a shrine or other holy place. Pilgrimages were popular in medieval times. Christians were taught that, in return for making the journey, Christ would forgive their sins. At the time of the Crusades, pilgrimages took weeks or months, and although they could occasionally be exciting, they were also exhausting and very dangerous. Jerusalem was holy for Christians because it was there that Jesus was crucified and rose from the dead. The city was also very important to Jews. For Muslims, the Dome of the Rock and other places in Jerusalem were sacred to their religion – Islam.

A PILGRIM BAND

Pilgrims usually travelled in groups or bands, for protection and companionship. In the 14th century, the English poet Geoffrey Chaucer wrote a long poem called *The Canterbury Tales* about a band of pilgrims on their way to the shrine of St Thomas Becket. As they set out from the Tabard Inn in London, they decided to tell stories to amuse themselves and help pass the time.

INDEPENDENT WOMAN
Women usually travelled in groups or with their husbands. This pilgrim is an exception.

MINSTREL
Musicians and other entertainers were always welcome on a long journey.

The barefoot pilgrim
Christian pilgrims were often shown carrying a purse and a sturdy wooden staff. The staff could be used to defend the traveller from attack by thieves. Pilgrims often made the last part of the journey on foot to show their humility.

MERCHANT
Most merchants were used to long journeys. Some chose to travel by land rather than sea because of the danger of pirates.

PEASANTS
Poorer pilgrims were sometimes given money by fellow travellers, or offered free accommodation.

SOLDIER
Armed guards travelled with the pilgrims on dangerous stretches of the journey.

NOBLES
Knights often travelled in luxury, accompanied by their servants.

This illuminated letter "B" is decorated using coloured pictures and borders.

Christ is shown saving people from the devil.

Symbols of faith

PILGRIMS WORE A BADGE to identify themselves and each pilgrimage site also had its own emblem. Pilgrims kept the badges as souvenirs to show friends and relatives.

Gours were used to hold wine or water.

A scallop-shell badge

The pilgrim's badge
Pilgrims to the shrine of St James at Compostella wore a badge of scallop shells. The symbol for Jerusalem was a palm leaf. One of the first guide books ever written was for pilgrims to Compostella. It was written by Aymeric, a French monk, in 1130.

VISIONS OF HELL
This detail from a 12th-century illuminated manuscript shows Jesus driving out devils. Fear of hell was a strong reason to go on a pilgrimage, especially for those who had lived a bad life and wanted God's forgiveness.

CANTERBURY
The tomb of Thomas Becket – the Archbishop of Canterbury at the time of King Henry II – was visited by pilgrims. Becket was murdered in 1170 in Canterbury cathedral. Three years later he was made a saint.

● Canterbury

JERUSALEM
The magnificent mosque, the Dome of the Rock, stands on the site where the prophet Mohammed is said to have ascended to heaven in the 7th century AD. The site is also sacred to Jews and Christians.

COMPOSTELLA
The 12th-century cathedral of Santiago de Compostella in Spain was built over the tomb of St James, one of Christ's apostles. It was an important place for Christian pilgrims in medieval times.

Compostella
●

Rome
●

● Jerusalem

● Mecca

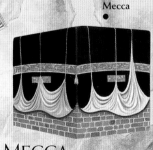

ROME
St Peter's basilica was built in the 16th century, near the spot where the apostle Peter, considered the first pope, was martyred in AD 67. Ever since, pilgrims have prayed at his tomb.

MECCA
For Muslims, Mecca in Saudi Arabia is the most important centre of pilgrimage. Muslim pilgrims pray at the Kaaba (House of God), said to have been built by Abraham and his son Ishmael.

PRIESTS
Most pilgrim bands included several holy people, such as priests, friars, or a prioress (nun), as in Chaucer's tale.

The First Crusade

Knights on horseback waited to board ships that would take them to the Holy Land.

WHEN RUMOURS REACHED EUROPE THAT the Muslim Seljuk Turks were stopping pilgrims from visiting Jerusalem, the Christian Church came up with the idea of a crusade or "Holy War". Knights who had spent much of their time fighting each other over land were now urged to defend Christianity.

The Venetians built ships with special doors and ramps in the bow for transporting horses.

Sailors loading the ship.

Bales of cloth, valuable to the crusaders, were used to trade for food, horses, and equipment.

"Anyone joining Louis [on crusade] need have no fear of Hell, for his soul will be in Paradise with the angels of Our Lord."

Chorus of medieval French crusader song

A colourful banner bore each knight's personal coat of arms and reserved his place in the ship.

A squire's job was to make sure that the knights' armour and weapons were stowed safely on board.

In this 14th-century manuscript painting, ships bound for the Holy Land are loaded with supplies for the crusader armies.

GOD WILLS IT!

ON 27TH NOVEMBER 1095, POPE URBAN II arrived in the French town of Clermont to make an important announcement. In those days it was rare for a pope to travel far from Rome, so a big crowd had gathered in a field outside the cathedral to hear him speak. Urban called for the people to take up arms in God's name and lead a crusade (holy war) against the Muslims. He claimed they were persecuting Christians and destroying shrines in the land where Christ had lived and died. As the people shouted, "God wills it!", Bishop Adhemar of Le Puy knelt at the feet of the Pope and became the first crusader.

> "Gird yourselves, I say, and act like mighty sons because it is better for you to die in battle than tolerate the abuse of your race and your holy places."
>
> Pope Urban II, at Clermont, 1095

Pope Urban II preached to the crowd outside the cathedral.

HEAVENLY REWARD

Every crusader took an oath vowing to fight on until Jerusalem and the other holy places were in Christian hands. In return, Pope Urban promised that Christ would forgive the knight's sins and reward him with a place in heaven if he died on the battlefield.

Gripped by enthusiasm, pilgrims tore up their cloaks to make crosses.

Peasants were eager to join the crusaders. Whole families left their homes to go on the pilgrimage.

Peter the Hermit

The People's Crusade was made up of ordinary men and women who set off for the Holy Land before the official leaving date. One of their leaders was Peter the Hermit, a fiery preacher who attracted thousands of followers in France and Germany. His sermons were so inspiring that some people were convinced he was a saint. Some believed that touching his cloak would cure illnesses, while others took hairs from his mule as souvenirs.

TAKING THE CROSS

The cross became the badge of the crusading movement and was worn proudly on the tunic of every crusader. People who joined the crusade were said to "take the cross". Urban wanted only knights and professional soldiers to volunteer for the holy war, but as word spread, ordinary men and women were inspired to go along too. Many left for the Holy Land months before the official departure date of 15th August 1096 and so were not protected by the main crusading armies.

THE FIRST VICTIMS

Some leaders of the People's Crusade were bloodthirsty fanatics. One of the worst was Emich of Leiningen, who terrorised the Jewish communities of the Rhineland, blaming them for Christ's death and likening them to the Muslims. In the spring of 1096, Emich took money from Jewish community leaders before encouraging his soldiers to kill Jews. To this day no one knows exactly how many Jews were massacred in this way.

Crusaders dipped their swords in animal blood to terrify the Jews.

Jewish homes were set on fire.

SORRY END

None of the unruly armies that made up the People's Crusade ever reached the Holy Land. Some were killed in clashes with Byzantine troops in Bulgaria, while others were massacred by the Turks in Anatolia. The remainder either went home dejected, or, like Peter the Hermit, waited to join the first official crusade.

The crusaders took few belongings with them and only a little food for the journey.

A rich man and his men join the march.

SELLING UP

Going on crusade was an expensive business for everyone. A wealthy nobleman might raise money by selling some of his property or renting out part of his estate. Poor people, on the other hand, were not so lucky. Some peasants sold their most precious possessions to the local monastery.

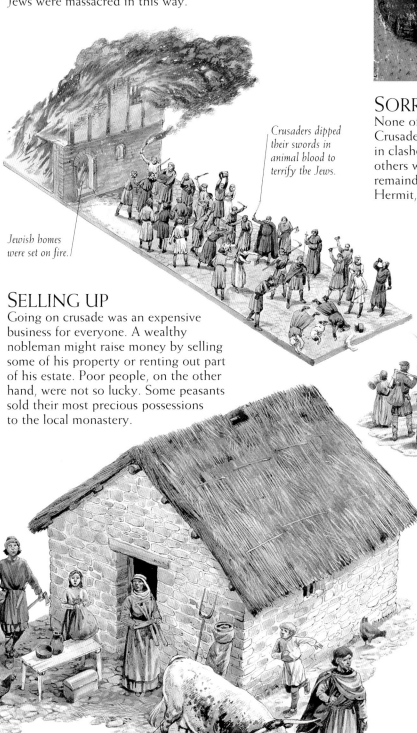

A cow could be sold to raise money for the journey.

HEADING EAST

Men, women, and children joined the crusade. All kinds of people – peasants, tradesmen, monks, nuns, criminals, and adventurers – set off. Many saw it as a chance to start a new life. Others wanted God's forgiveness, believing that the world was about to end.

FACT file

• Pope Urban was on the road for 13 months (August 1095–September 1096). He preached in more than 40 French towns and cities, and was accompanied by two cardinals, four archbishops, and five bishops.

• At least 800 Jews were massacred in Worms, Germany. Some of their graves can still be seen outside the cathedral.

THE TABLES ARE TURNED

2 June 1098

Almost a year after the Battle of Dorylaeum the crusaders captured Antioch. They in turn were besieged by the army of the Turkish warlord, Kerbogha. Worse still, they knew they could not hold out for long because they had little food.

BETRAYAL
Antioch was only captured after a Turkish guard let the crusaders in.

TORTOISE

As the attackers approached the wall, they raised their shields above their heads, creating a protective shell. This manoeuvre was known as the *testudo* (Latin for tortoise).

The interlocking shields sheltered the attackers from the rain of arrows.

Antioch

The main crusader army marched to Jerusalem.

CHRIST'S ARMY

28 June 1098

After fighting their way out of Antioch, the crusaders marched on to Jerusalem. They were inspired by the "Holy Lance", the spear which, they believed, had pierced Christ's side on the cross. The lance was one of many relics (sacred objects) carried by the warrior pilgrims.

Crusaders

Turks

Genoese ships were broken up for wood.

Timber was carted to Jerusalem.

OUTSIDE DORYLAEUM

1 July 1097

As the crusader army approached the city of Dorylaeum, the Turks surrounded the advance guard. Crusader reinforcements soon arrived and the battle grew fiercer. Last on the scene was Bishop Adhemar of Le Puy, who ordered his men to set fire to the Turks' camp, forcing them to flee.

TO JERUSALEM

IT WOULD HAVE TAKEN MOST pilgrims several months to make the journey from Constantinople to Jerusalem. For the crusading armies it was more than two years' hard travelling. Thousands of men and women died along the way – from hunger, disease, and heat exhaustion, as well as in battle. When their horses collapsed, the once-proud knights were forced to ride on mules or continue the journey on foot, dragging their armour with them. Not surprisingly many crusaders were tempted to go home, including Peter the Hermit, who was caught and led back to camp. To add to their troubles, the crusaders had to fight for more than 10 months to capture the fortified Turkish cities of Nicaea and Antioch. The crusaders put up with these hardships, in the hope that one day they would see the "Holy City".

Marching south

From Constantinople the crusaders marched through Anatolia (now Turkey) until they reached the Syrian border. Here, a small force led by Count Baldwin of Boulogne broke away to capture Edessa, which became the first crusader state. The main crusader army laid siege to the town of Antioch before heading south, to Jerusalem.

Siege warfare

This painting by William of Tyre shows the siege of Antioch in 1097. Laying siege to a town or castle was the most important part of medieval warfare. It involved continual attacks until the people inside the town or castle surrendered.

19 June 1097 **TAKING NICAEA**

For seven weeks and three days the crusading armies besieged the city of Nicaea without success. When their ally, the Byzantine emperor Alexius, sent reinforcements and the city surrendered, he claimed all the glory. This made the crusaders furious.

CATAPULTS
When the crusaders ran out of rocks to hurl over the walls, they loaded their catapults with the heads of dead Turks.

FISHING FOR BODIES
The Turks hauled the bodies of dead crusaders up to the ramparts and stole their armour.

Nicaea

OCCUPYING FORCE
Alexius wanted to keep Nicaea under his rule, so he paid off the crusaders with gold and supplies. He ordered his troops to stay behind in Nicaea to prevent the Turks recapturing it.

Routes to the same destination
The crusaders took three different routes to Constantinople. One army travelled through Hungary, while another followed the northern Adriatic coast. The third army passed through Italy to Dürres, and travelled across Byzantine territory.

ON THE ROAD

BY THE SUMMER OF 1096, THE crusaders were starting out on their great adventure. Three main armies travelled across Europe to Constantinople. The largest was commanded by Count Raymond of Toulouse and his advisor, Bishop Adhemar. (Adhemar's secretary Raymond of Aguilers, later wrote an account of their terrible journey.) One army was led by Godfrey of Bouillon. It marched through Hungary, where the King held Godfrey's brother Baldwin and his family hostage as a way to guarantee the crusaders' good behaviour. The third army went through Italy, where they were blessed by Pope Urban and prayed at St Peter's tomb in Rome.

A horse was a knight's most valuable possession.

The long oars were used to help steer the boat.

SIDE BY SIDE
Priests and monks accompanied the crusaders on their journey. As well as preaching sermons, they called on God to bless the men and women on their holy mission. Fear of death made even the rowdiest crusaders pay attention!

BOAT CROSSING
For the third army, the boat crossing from Italy took four days and was very uncomfortable. Passengers slept on wooden planks below deck, where tar stuck to their clothing. Travellers who were not seasick amused themselves by getting drunk, hunting for rats, or picking the lice from their bodies.

FORAGING
As the crusaders marched east, they found fewer people ready to welcome foreigners tramping through their land. Soldiers asking for food and drink were turned away even when they offered money. In desperation, some of the crusaders stole from farms and villages as they passed.

Robbers attacked crusaders and stole their possessions.

Desperate for food, some crusaders hunted wild animals in the hills.

> "For three weeks we saw neither wild beasts nor birds. The barbarous and ignorant natives would neither trade with us nor provide guides."
>
> Written by Raymond of Aguilers c. 1100

Some crusaders exchanged gold or jewellery for provisions (food). They were worth more to the merchants than European coins.

THIRSTY WORK

The crusaders were unprepared for the extreme differences in climate as they journeyed east. Summer temperatures in Greece and the Middle East were 6°C (11°F) higher on average than in Northern Europe. In summer, thousands of soldiers suffered from dehydration. In winter, freezing rain made food rot and mail rust.

Knights in heavy armour suffered from heatstroke. For them it was like sitting inside a furnace.

The crusaders bought fruit and vegetables from market traders along the route.

SCARING TARANTULAS

Large spiders called tarantulas – which have a poisonous bite – lurked under rocks in this part of the world. To frighten them away, the crusaders banged on shields and pans.

MARKET FORCES

Market traders in the East knew the crusaders were desperate for food and so they charged high prices. Also, there were no fixed exchange rates, as there are today, so traders could decide for themselves how much a coin was worth.

DESPERATE MEASURES

Very little grows in the dry rocky centre of Anatolia (now Turkey). The crusaders quenched their thirst with moisture from prickly desert shrubs.

KEEPING SPIRITS UP

Music helped the soldiers forget their aching feet and rumbling stomachs. Wandering minstrels, called troubadours, sang songs called "Wonderful Jerusalem" and "Knights, your salvation is assured", accompanying themselves on drums and trumpets. The pilgrims also made up their own songs about life on the road.

Troubadours

FACT file

• During the dangerous sea crossing from Brindisi in Italy to Dürres in Albania, one of the transport ships capsized in a storm. Four hundred men and women were drowned.

• Many horses and donkeys perished crossing the desert. Carts were pulled by dogs and knights were forced to ride oxen.

Taking Jerusalem

When the crusaders finally reached Jerusalem in June 1099, the Turkish army was ready for them. For weeks the defenders had been storing up food so that nothing was left for the Christians to find. There were also rumours that the wells outside the city had been poisoned. The crusaders began attacking straight away, but made little progress until the siege towers were ready on 14th July. The following morning they stormed the Turkish defences and entered the city in triumph.

STORMING THE WALLS

14 July 1099

Under cover of darkness the crusaders' siege towers were moved into position and, at daybreak, the assault began. The fierce fighting lasted all day and was followed by a night of tense watchfulness on both sides. When the battle started again the next morning, the first crusaders managed to leap over the city walls.

SIEGE TOWERS
Tall wooden siege towers were wheeled right up to the city walls. The troops on the top crossed to the battlements using a makeshift drawbridge.

FIRST IN
Godfrey of Bouillon and his men were the first to fight their way into Jerusalem.

Outside Antioch, Kerbogha's army were defeated by the crusaders.

DRY CROSSING
The dry moat was filled with boulders so that the crusaders could reach the walls. For every three stones they collected, volunteers were paid one silver coin.

EXPLOSION!
The Turks fought back with "Greek fire" – pots filled with flammable sulphur, resins, and oils, which exploded like a bomb on landing.

Jerusalem

SHIPS TO THE RESCUE
There was a shortage of trees in the dry, rocky terrain. The crusaders used wood from Genoese supply ships to make siege machinery for the attack on Jerusalem.

BEFORE THE BATTLE

8 July 1099

A week before they breached the walls of Jerusalem, the crusaders paraded barefoot around the city walls, carrying relics and praying to God for courage. The Turks looked down in amazement, shouting abuse at them.

BATTERING RAM
The crusaders used massive tree trunks as battering rams to weaken the walls. These huge machines also sheltered the soldiers from enemy attack.

15 July 1099 — TANCRED'S DASH FOR GOLD

Tancred, a 21-year-old Norman crusader knight, led his excited followers through the city to the Dome of the Rock. Thousands of terrified Muslims had gathered inside the mosque to pray for rescue. When they heard the soldiers shouting, they fled to the nearby al-Aqsa mosque, leaving Tancred and his men to plunder the treasures of the Dome.

16 July 1099 — BROKEN PROMISE

Tancred had promised to protect the Muslims sheltering in the al-Aqsa mosque, but the following morning they were massacred by the crusaders. The Jews suffered a similar fate when the synagogue in which they were hiding was burnt to the ground, killing all the people inside.

WADING IN BLOOD
The crusaders rampaged through the city, killing everyone in sight. In the end the soldiers had to climb over piles of bodies.

GOLDEN DOME
On the Temple Mount stood the Dome of the Rock, built over the place that Christians, Jews, and Muslims believed was sacred to their religion.

GLITTERING PRIZES
Crusader soldiers returned to camp, carrying food and booty. Among the treasures looted from the Dome of the Rock were hundreds of gold and silver candelabras and a great silver lamp.

GRUESOME BOOTY

As well as looting mosques and houses, the crusaders ripped open the bodies of dead Turks, searching for gold coins. It was rumoured that they had swallowed the coins in haste when the battle began.

When the Turks lowered bales of straw to absorb the shock from the battering rams, the crusaders set fire to them.

> "Everywhere lay fragments of human bodies, and the very ground was covered with the blood of the slain."
>
> William of Tyre, 12th–century historian

FACT file

- During the Siege of Antioch, the crusaders' menu was as follows:– a tongueless horse's head cost three gold coins, goats' intestines cost five coins, an egg was worth two coins, and the price of a chicken was three coins.

- Only a third of the crusaders who reached Constantinople early in 1097 survived to fight at Jerusalem. This number included fewer than 1,500 knights.

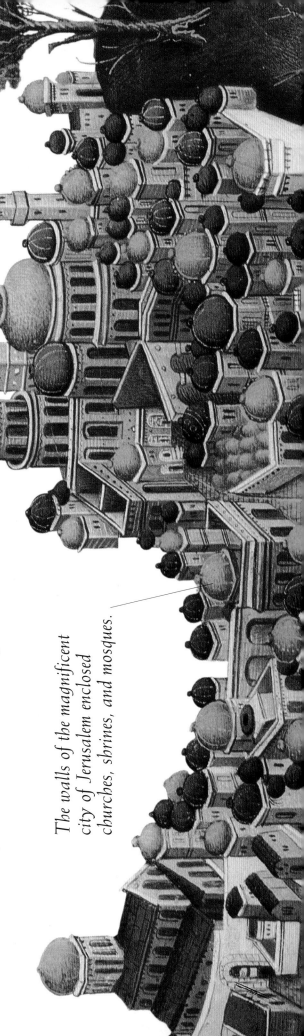

The Settlement

> "Those who were strangers are now natives and he who was a sojourner [visitor] now has become a resident."
>
> Fulcher of Chartres, a
> 12th-century chronicler

A 14th-century
view of Jerusalem

WITH THE CAPTURE OF JERUSALEM, MOST OF the crusaders felt they had fulfilled their promise and were now free to return to Europe. However, a small number decided to stay and settle in the East. These Europeans controlled much of the Holy Land (known to the settlers as Outremer) for the next 200 years.

*The walls of the magnificent
city of Jerusalem enclosed
churches, shrines, and mosques.*

Pennant

Follow the leader
In the confusion of battle it was easy to become separated from your leader. These 11th-century knights follow the pennant of their lord, which marks him out on the battlefield. When heraldry was introduced, nobles used large banners displaying their coats of arms, so everyone could easily spot their lord.

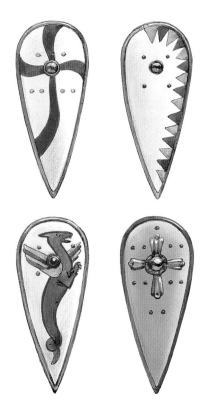

Badges of recognition
These 11th-century shields have designs to help soldiers recognise their owner. In the 12th century, true heraldry was developed, at first probably to identify knights in tournaments. Soon all knights wore a family badge on their shields. From the mid-12th century, knights began to wear a cloth surcoat bearing their coat of arms over their armour.

KNIGHTS AND CASTLES

A KNIGHT BEGAN HIS TRAINING AS a page at an early age. Pages spent much of their childhood learning how to ride and handle weapons. When a page was about 14 years old he was promoted to squire (apprentice knight) and was allowed to accompany his lord into battle. He was now a member of a team, which may have included a few foot soldiers, such as archers, and a groom who looked after the horses and pack mules. A knight usually fought on horseback. For protection he wore a hauberk (a long tunic made of mail) with a mail coif, or hood. Helmets were not always worn at this time. The armour could be stifling, especially in Syria and Anatolia, where temperatures reached 40°C (85°F). Some crusaders began to wear a loose-fitting cloth coat to stop sunlight hitting their armour and making them hotter.

Archers marched behind the knight.

Foot soldiers wore padded tunics.

Lance

GOING INTO BATTLE
When knights rode into battle, they were often protected by a ring of foot soldiers. At a given signal, the ring of soldiers parted and the knights charged, each one holding his lance "couched" (tucked under his right armpit) and his shield and reins in his left hand. He plunged the lance into the body of his Saracen opponent with such force that without a special, high-backed saddle he would have been flung from his seat.

Double-edged sword blade

WAR SWORD

All knights carried a sword. The crusader's weapon was made from a mixture of iron and steel. It was double-edged, enabling him to slash at the enemy from side to side. From the end of the 13th century, swords that tapered to a sharp point were often used. Thickening them down the centre made them stiff, ideal for thrusting through mail armour.

A cross-guard protected the knight's hand.

DEADLY CROSSBOW

The crossbow was an accurate and powerful weapon. It shot bolts with barbed tips capable of going through mail. One crusader was saved from certain death when the bolt that had pierced his armour bounced off a locket he was wearing around his neck.

Crossbow

Wooden tiller   Crossbow bolts

Castle building

SAONE CASTLE NEAR ANTIOCH was one of a network of crusader fortresses built in the 12th century. It stands on a rocky spur (ridge) with clear views of the Syrian countryside. The castle was used mainly as a garrison for soldiers and for storing food and military supplies. Officials also worked at the castle, collecting taxes, making laws, and settling disputes for the local lord.

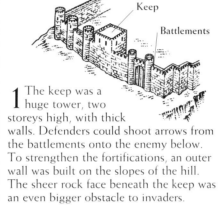

Keep

Battlements

1 The keep was a huge tower, two storeys high, with thick walls. Defenders could shoot arrows from the battlements onto the enemy below. To strengthen the fortifications, an outer wall was built on the slopes of the hill. The sheer rock face beneath the keep was an even bigger obstacle to invaders.

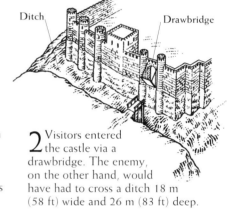

Ditch

Drawbridge

2 Visitors entered the castle via a drawbridge. The enemy, on the other hand, would have had to cross a ditch 18 m (58 ft) wide and 26 m (83 ft) deep.

Curved sabre

Round shield

Saracen archer

SARACENS

Like Christian knights, Saracens fought on horseback, carrying long lances, sabres, maces (clubs), and daggers. Mounted Saracen archers swooped down and shot at the enemy before galloping away. Their deadly shower of arrows left a trail of destruction.

Pigeon post
Even in peacetime Muslim commanders used homing pigeons to carry messages. They became vitally important when armies were trapped in a besieged city and needed to make contact with rescuing forces. If, on the other hand, the crusaders managed to shoot the pigeons down, they could quickly find out what the enemy was up to. Drums and smoke signals were other ways of communicating with friendly armies camped nearby.

GOD'S ARMIES

FROM ABOUT 1110, NEW MILITARY orders (armies of knights) were formed to defend Outremer. The best of these troops were the Hospitallers and the Templars. The Hospitallers were also known as the Knights of St John, and they ran a hospital for pilgrims in Jerusalem. The Templars built their headquarters on the site of the ancient Jewish temple in the city. The knights ate together and attended religious services, just like monks. They dedicated their lives to God and vowed to fight the "infidel" (non-Christians). The Hospitallers and Templars obeyed their own leaders, called the Grand Masters.

MARIENBURG
From 1309, the headquarters of the Teutonic Order was Marienburg Castle on the River Vistula (now in Poland). Rich knights from all over Europe joined annual winter campaigns fighting against the non-Christian Lithuanians in return for land and riches.

France and Auvergne

England

Germany

Jerusalem

Coats of arms
On the islands of Rhodes and Malta, Hospitallers from different countries lived in separate hostels called auberges. Each auberge had its own coat of arms over the door, which can still be seen today. The kingdom of Jerusalem also had a coat of arms.

EXPANDING ARMIES
This map shows the spread of the military orders throughout Europe and the Middle East. The Teutonic Knights, were another new order who, like the Hospitallers, ran a hospital in Outremer. The Spaniards set up several military orders of their own to defend Christianity in Spain. One of these, the Order of Calatrava, fought the Muslim Moors in Granada, Spain until 1492.

The Hospitallers were based in Malta from 1530-1798.

Malta

VALLETTA
In 1530 the Hospitallers used Malta as a base for their continuing battles with the Turks. The capital of the island, Valletta, is named after Jean de la Vallete, the Grand Master who built a fortress there in 1565.

FACT file
• Most Templars and Hospitallers joined the orders in their mid-twenties. According to records, the youngest volunteer was 10 years old.
• Even though the military orders became wealthy and powerful, they did not abandon their important work of looking after the pilgrims.

HOSPITALLERS
Founded in 1113, the Knights of St John helped to look after sick and injured pilgrims. Their hospital in Jerusalem took care of up to 200 patients and had its own physicians and surgeons. There was even a ward with cots for babies born on the pilgrimage.

The Assassins

A scarf was worn to hide the face.

BASED IN CASTLES in Syria, the Assassins were a private army of Shi'ite Muslims. Their main enemies were Sunni Muslims, but they killed Christians too.

Fierce killers
The Assassins, founded by Hasan-i Sabbah, carried out religious killings for money. Wearing a disguise or covering their faces to avoid detection, they stabbed their victims to death using a knife or dagger.

Dagger for stabbing victims.

The Teutonic Order moved to Marienburg in eastern Germany in 1309.

ENGLAND

GERMANY

● Marienburg

The headquarters of the Teutonic Order was in Venice from 1291–1309.

● Venice

HUNGARY

The Hospitallers settled in Rhodes in 1306. Three years later the town became their headquarters.

Rhodes

Cyprus

The Hospitallers and Templars operated from Cyprus from 1291–1309.

Acre ●

In 1291, the military orders were forced out of Acre – their last base in Outremer – by the Saracens.

● Jerusalem

RHODES
The headquarters of the Hospitallers was in Rhodes. The knights built a harbour and a castle with fortified towers. The town walls enclosed a hospital, Grand Master's Palace, church, arsenal (weapons store), and knights' hostels.

St. John Ambulance
The charitable work started by the Order of St John continues today in organisations like the St John Ambulance service. There are now more than 300,000 members in 42 countries. In some countries, children become volunteers and are taught first aid and emergency procedures.

TEUTONIC KNIGHTS
The German Teutonic Knights soon turned their attention from defending the Holy Land to attacking the non-Christian people of Prussia, Lithuania, and Livonia (Latvia). They came back with wagonloads of loot, cattle, and horses. To some people they were invaders rather than holy warriors.

TEMPLARS
In 1129 the Pope made the Templars a special religious order. They took vows of obedience and promised to defend the Holy Land. In return, the Templars were allowed to wear linen instead of wool in the intense heat of Outremer. In 1307, the Templars in France were arrested. Perhaps the king was jealous of their wealth. The Grand Master, Jacques de Molay, was burnt at the stake in 1314, protesting the Order's innocence to the end.

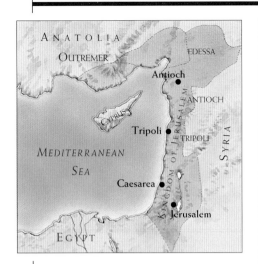

Crusader towns and territories
After the capture of Jerusalem in 1099, the crusaders set about strengthening their hold on Outremer. By 1140 they controlled a long strip of land stretching from the mountains of Anatolia (now Turkey) to the border of Egypt.

Queen Melisande's psalter
A beautifully illustrated psalter (book of psalms) was made for Melisande, Queen of Jerusalem, 1131–43. Melisande loved fine things and invited the best craftsmen in Europe to come to Outremer to build new monasteries and cathedrals for the Christian community.

CAESAREA

The port of Caesarea was captured by the crusaders in 1101. It was typical of the crusader settlements in Outremer. First, the crusaders turned the Muslim mosque into a Christian church. Later, they built a cathedral in the town. The settlers became rich through trading, and because the land beyond the gates of the town was so fertile. Vineyards and orchards were planted along with crops of beans, chickpeas, sugar cane, and barley.

LIFE IN OUTREMER

THE CRUSADERS CALLED THE LAND THEY had conquered Outremer, which means "beyond the sea". The crusader leaders divided the land into three areas (Edessa, Tripoli, and Antioch), which were all part of the kingdom of Jerusalem. For a time the crusaders in Outremer stayed separate from their Muslim neighbours. However, later generations of Christians born in Outremer began to adopt Arab customs, such as using soap and wearing turbans. While European visitors to Outremer still looked on Muslims as their enemies, the residents of Outremer saw them as friends and trading partners.

ORCHARDS

Citrus fruits flourished in the sunny climate of Outremer. Following the harvest, refreshing drinks were made from the juice of oranges and lemons.

Citrus fruit

Small farm

The town of Caesarea, c. 1150

THE MARKET

Arabic markets were social centres as well as shops. The men came for a shave or a haircut, to play a game of dice, or to chat with friends over a plate of lamb and bean stew.

30

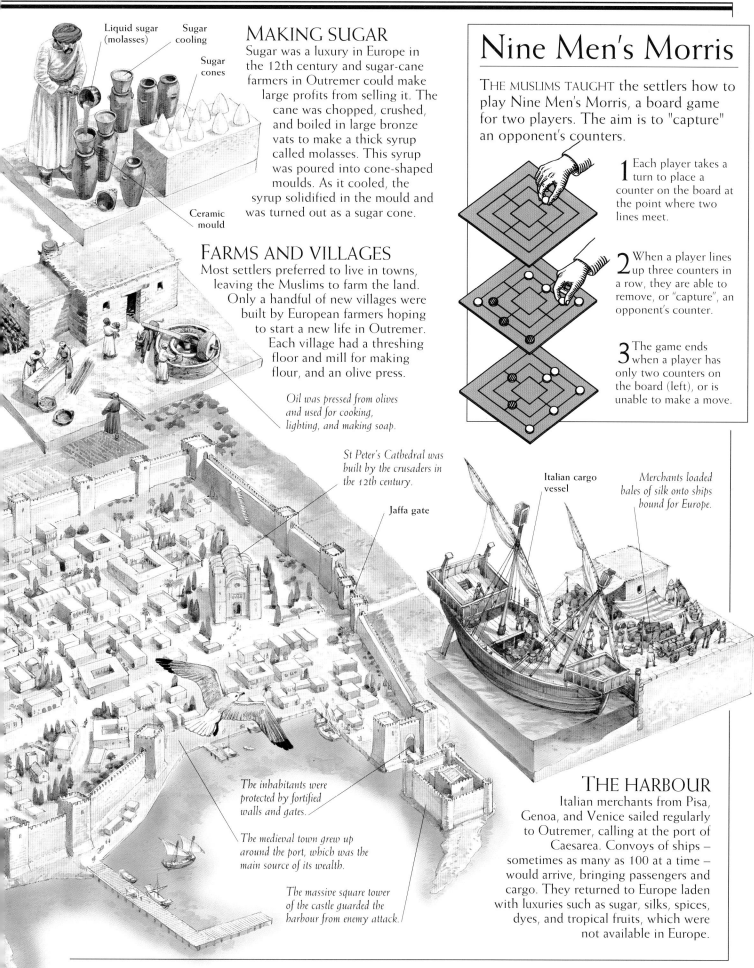

MAKING SUGAR

Liquid sugar (molasses)

Sugar cooling

Sugar cones

Ceramic mould

Sugar was a luxury in Europe in the 12th century and sugar-cane farmers in Outremer could make large profits from selling it. The cane was chopped, crushed, and boiled in large bronze vats to make a thick syrup called molasses. This syrup was poured into cone-shaped moulds. As it cooled, the syrup solidified in the mould and was turned out as a sugar cone.

FARMS AND VILLAGES

Most settlers preferred to live in towns, leaving the Muslims to farm the land. Only a handful of new villages were built by European farmers hoping to start a new life in Outremer. Each village had a threshing floor and mill for making flour, and an olive press.

Oil was pressed from olives and used for cooking, lighting, and making soap.

St Peter's Cathedral was built by the crusaders in the 12th century.

Jaffa gate

The inhabitants were protected by fortified walls and gates.

The medieval town grew up around the port, which was the main source of its wealth.

The massive square tower of the castle guarded the harbour from enemy attack.

Nine Men's Morris

THE MUSLIMS TAUGHT the settlers how to play Nine Men's Morris, a board game for two players. The aim is to "capture" an opponent's counters.

1 Each player takes a turn to place a counter on the board at the point where two lines meet.

2 When a player lines up three counters in a row, they are able to remove, or "capture", an opponent's counter.

3 The game ends when a player has only two counters on the board (left), or is unable to make a move.

Italian cargo vessel

Merchants loaded bales of silk onto ships bound for Europe.

THE HARBOUR

Italian merchants from Pisa, Genoa, and Venice sailed regularly to Outremer, calling at the port of Caesarea. Convoys of ships – sometimes as many as 100 at a time – would arrive, bringing passengers and cargo. They returned to Europe laden with luxuries such as sugar, silks, spices, dyes, and tropical fruits, which were not available in Europe.

Like the crusaders, Saracen warriors carried colourful banners into battle. As the cavalry charged, their pennants fluttered in the breeze.

Muslim soldiers fought to the sound of horns, tabors (small drums), and kettledrums.

A celebration of the end of the Muslim festival of Ramadan, illustrated by Hariri in the 13th-century manuscript called, "The Ma'qawat" (Meetings).

The End of the Dream

H OLDING ON TO OUTREMER PROVED FAR more difficult than the crusaders had expected. By the end of the 12th century, the Muslims had sorted out their differences and were united by a new determination, while the European princes were falling out over land and loot. Meanwhile the Christian Church was urging crusaders to join "holy wars" closer to home – in Europe.

The Muslim cavalry used Arab horses that were bred for speed. They were smaller and lighter than the crusaders' mounts.

> " "A year later I crossed the battlefield and saw the land still covered with their bones. They could be seen even from a distance, lying in heaps or scattered around."
>
> Ibn al-Athir, at Hattin, 1188 "

THE MUSLIMS FIGHT BACK

THE MUSLIMS WERE SHOCKED BY THE capture of Jerusalem and massacre of its inhabitants. Gradually they began a campaign to recover their lands from the Christians. On Christmas Eve, 1144, the governor of Mosul, Imad al-Din Zengi, seized Edessa from the crusaders. His son, Nur al-Din took control of Egypt and called for *jihad*, or holy war, against the Christians. The man who united the Muslim forces was Saladin, who became ruler of Egypt in 1169. By 1185, his empire surrounded most of the crusader lands. On 4th July 1187, Saladin's army met the crusaders on the battlefield of Hattin.

"I cried out in joy: 'We have beaten them'. My father turned to me and said: 'Be silent. We shall not defeat them until that [red] tent [of the king] falls'. As he spoke, the tent fell."

The Battle of Hattin, descibed by Saladin's son, al-Afdal 'Ali, c. 1187

Capture of Kerak Castle
Between 1187 and 1189 Saladin took 50 crusader castles and much of the crusader kingdom. However, even his enemies thought him chivalrous. During the siege of Kerak he refused to bombard a tower in which a honeymoon couple was staying. He also returned a child, captured for slavery, to its crusader mother.

BATTLE PLANS
Saladin brought about 30,000 men across the River Jordan. He sent part of the army to the town of Tiberias, hoping to lure the Christian army from its camp nearby at Sephorie. His plan worked. Guy of Lusignan, king of Jerusalem, led about 20,000 crusaders towards the Muslims at Tiberias. Saladin's army watched and waited.

30 June 1187

A THIRSTY MARCH
The crusaders, led by King Guy, set out from their camp on 3rd July, heading for Tiberias. On the way, they were involved in skirmishes with the Muslims, their horses were shot down by arrows, and they suffered from the heat.

Castle at Tiberias

IN HIDING
The crusader region of Galilee was ruled from Tiberias by Raymond of Tripoli. When the town was captured by Saladin's army, Raymond's wife hid in the castle until after the battle.

Lake Tiberias

Tiberias

HORNS OF HATTIN
Hattin was in the middle of the Kingdom of Jerusalem. A double hill outside the town was known as Qarn Hattin (the Horns of Hattin).

SPLITTING FORCES
Saladin's and his men camped at Cafarsset. He sent part of his army to blockade Tiberias, then, with the rest of his soldiers, he set out to besiege the city.

Horns of Hattin

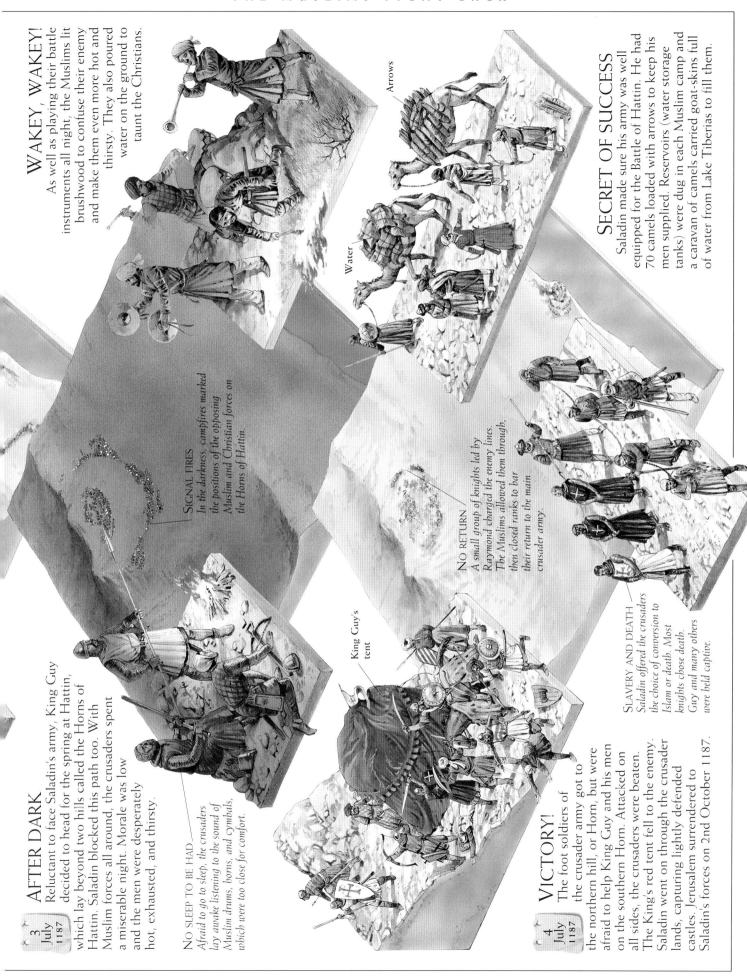

WAKEY, WAKEY!

As well as playing their battle instruments all night, the Muslims lit brushwood to confuse their enemy and make them even more hot and thirsty. They also poured water on the ground to taunt the Christians.

Arrows

Water

SECRET OF SUCCESS

Saladin made sure his army was well equipped for the Battle of Hattin. He had 70 camels loaded with arrows to keep his men supplied. Reservoirs (water storage tanks) were dug in each Muslim camp and a caravan of camels carried goat-skins full of water from Lake Tiberias to fill them.

SIGNAL FIRES
In the darkness, campfires marked the positions of the opposing Muslim and Christian forces on the Horns of Hattin.

NO RETURN
A small group of knights led by Raymond charged the enemy lines. The Muslims allowed them through, then closed ranks to bar their return to the main crusader army.

3
July
1187

AFTER DARK

Reluctant to face Saladin's army, King Guy decided to head for the spring at Hattin, which lay beyond two hills called the Horns of Hattin. Saladin blocked this path too. With Muslim forces all around, the crusaders spent a miserable night. Morale was low and the men were desperately hot, exhausted, and thirsty.

NO SLEEP TO BE HAD
Afraid to go to sleep, the crusaders lay awake listening to the sound of Muslim drums, horns, and cymbals, which were too close for comfort.

King Guy's tent

SLAVERY AND DEATH
Saladin offered the crusaders the choice of conversion to Islam or death. Most knights chose death. Guy and many others were held captive.

4
July
1187

VICTORY!

The foot soldiers of the crusader army got to the northern hill, or Horn, but were afraid to help King Guy and his men on the southern Horn. Attacked on all sides, the crusaders were beaten. The King's red tent fell to the enemy. Saladin went on through the crusader lands, capturing lightly defended castles. Jerusalem surrendered to Saladin's forces on 2nd October 1187.

Richard's wax seal was stamped on important documents.

Richard I of England
Historians agree that Richard – pictured here on his seal – was a natural soldier. Physically strong, brave, and fiery, he seemed to deserve his nickname, *"Coeur de Lion"* ("Lionheart"). Richard's closest ally had always been Philip II of France, but when the French king decided to return home after the fall of Acre, Richard was worried. He feared that Philip would take advantage of his absence and try to take his land in Normandy and Aquitaine.

The lost crusader
German Emperor Frederick Barbarossa (nicknamed "Redbeard") was the most powerful ruler of his day. He led one of the largest crusading armies ever gathered together, although it quickly disbanded. In June 1190, Frederick reached the banks of the fast-flowing River Calycadnus in Anatolia (now Turkey). As he tried to cross in full armour, he was thrown from his horse and drowned in the freezing water. His troops saw his death as a bad sign and many returned home.

CRUSADE OF THE KINGS

Losing Jerusalem to the Saracens was a blow to Christian pride. The Pope lost no time in appealing to the main European leaders to head another crusade. Emperor Frederick Barbarossa of Germany was the first to leave. A year later, in 1190, Richard of England and Philip of France met to plan a joint campaign. Both kings travelled by sea to the Holy Land, but Richard was diverted to Cyprus when his sister and her fiancée were shipwrecked and held hostage there. This was Richard's excuse to conquer Cyprus, which became an important base for later crusades. After marrying Berengaria, the daughter of the King of Navarre, Richard rejoined Philip to capture Acre in July 1191.

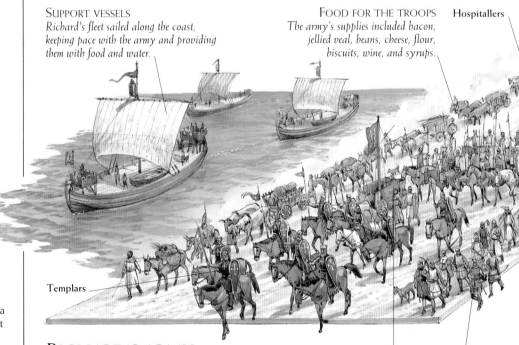

SUPPORT VESSELS
Richard's fleet sailed along the coast, keeping pace with the army and providing them with food and water.

FOOD FOR THE TROOPS
The army's supplies included bacon, jellied veal, beans, cheese, flour, biscuits, wine, and syrups.

Hospitallers

Templars

RICHARD'S ARMY
Even Richard's Saracen opponent, Saladin, was impressed by the discipline and courage of the crusading army. During battles, Richard's best troops, the Templars and Hospitallers, protected the army at the front and rear. These two bands stood firm whenever the Saracens tried to draw them into deadly ambushes.

MARCHING ORDER
The infantry marched on either side of the royal standard, or banner, which was mounted on a wooden cart.

PROTECTIVE ARROWS
The heavy cavalry was protected by crossbowmen, who marched on the flanks (sides) of the column.

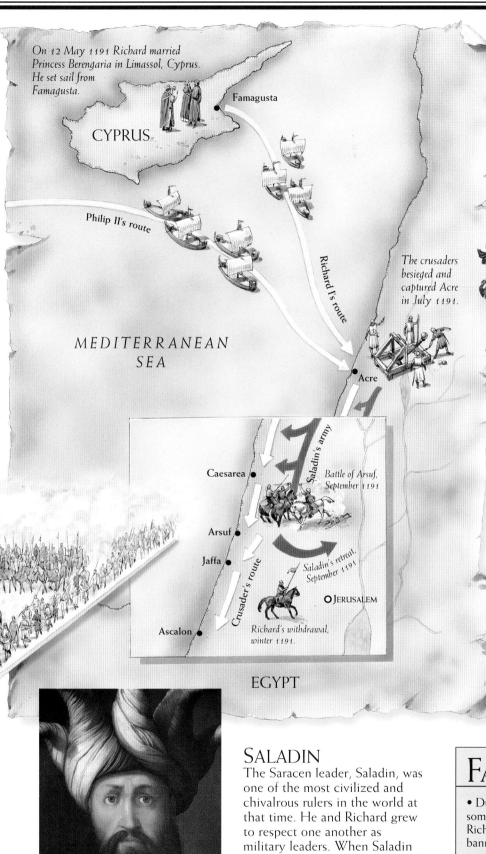

On 12 May 1191 Richard married Princess Berengaria in Limassol, Cyprus. He set sail from Famagusta.

CYPRUS

Famagusta

Philip II's route

Richard I's route

The crusaders besieged and captured Acre in July 1191.

MEDITERRANEAN SEA

Acre

Caesarea

Saladin's army

Battle of Arsuf, September 1191

Arsuf

Jaffa

Crusader's route

Saladin's retreat, September 1191

JERUSALEM

Ascalon

Richard's withdrawal, winter 1191.

EGYPT

RICHARD'S MARCH

After Acre, Philip returned to France. Richard and his army marched on and captured Arsuf, despite being harrassed by Saladin's forces. They continued to Jaffa, an important stronghold on the way to Jerusalem. Then, instead of heading for Jerusalem, Richard's exhausted army withdrew to Ascalon.

CALLING A TRUCE

Saladin and Richard realised that neither side could capture Jerusalem and win a total victory, so they agreed to a truce. The two rulers never did joust, as shown in this 13th-century illustration, but both were expert horsemen.

BAD NEIGHBOUR

Outside Acre, the crusaders constructed huge siege engines (shown above). These were given nicknames, such as "God's Own Sling" and "Bad Neighbour".

SALADIN

The Saracen leader, Saladin, was one of the most civilized and chivalrous rulers in the world at that time. He and Richard grew to respect one another as military leaders. When Saladin heard that Richard had fallen ill in Ascalon, he sent peaches and pears to help restore him to health. He also sent packs of snow from Mount Hermann to cool the King's fever.

FACT file

• Duke Leopold of Austria tried to take some of the credit for capturing Acre. Richard was furious and hurled Leopold's banner into a ditch. The Duke later got his revenge by imprisoning Richard and demanding a large ransom for his release.

• The Saracens built their own siege device, called "Bad Relative", in response to the crusaders' siege engines.

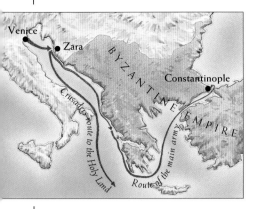

Venice
Zara
BYZANTINE EMPIRE
Constantinople
Crusader route to the Holy Land
Route of the main army

The Fourth Crusade
Though bound for Egypt, the Fourth Crusade first captured the Hungarian town of Zara. The main army then made for Constantinople. Other crusaders went to the Holy Land.

VENICE ARSENAL

In 1104, all the shipyards of the Venice lagoon were brought together into one large building called the Arsenal (ammunition store). It included a ship's "hard", or area for mooring vessels, and a ropewalk – a long shed used for twisting long ropes for ships' rigging.

SEIZING CONSTANTINOPLE

IN 1198, POPE INNOCENT III CALLED FOR a new crusade. The target was to be Egypt, a stronghold of Muslim power on the southeast coast of the Mediterranean. Dandolo, Doge (ruler) of the state of Venice, agreed to provide ships to take the crusaders to Egypt. In return, the crusader leaders agreed to recapture the town of Zara for the Venetians as payment for the ships. The crusaders were also promised help from the Byzantine ruler Alexius IV in return for restoring him and his father as co-emperors in Constantinople. As soon as the crusaders agreed to this deal, events took an unexpected turn. The Fourth Crusade never reached Egypt.

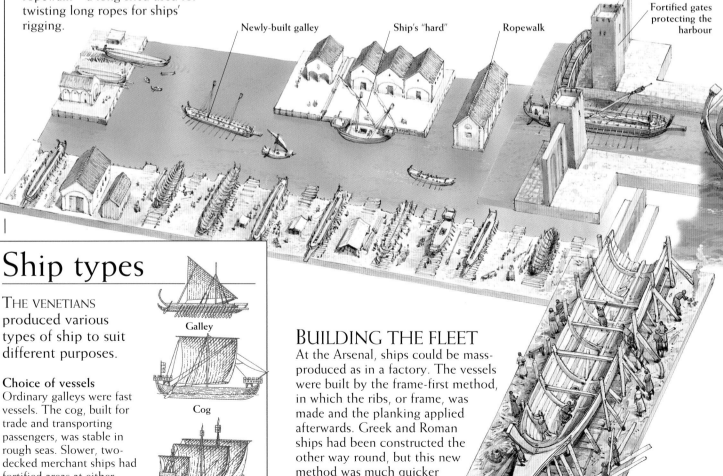

Newly-built galley

Ship's "hard"

Ropewalk

Fortified gates protecting the harbour

Ship types

THE VENETIANS produced various types of ship to suit different purposes.

Galley

Choice of vessels
Ordinary galleys were fast vessels. The cog, built for trade and transporting passengers, was stable in rough seas. Slower, two-decked merchant ships had fortified areas at either end. Ships for transporting horses were also used.

Cog

Two-decked ship

BUILDING THE FLEET

At the Arsenal, ships could be mass-produced as in a factory. The vessels were built by the frame-first method, in which the ribs, or frame, was made and the planking applied afterwards. Greek and Roman ships had been constructed the other way round, but this new method was much quicker and saved wood.

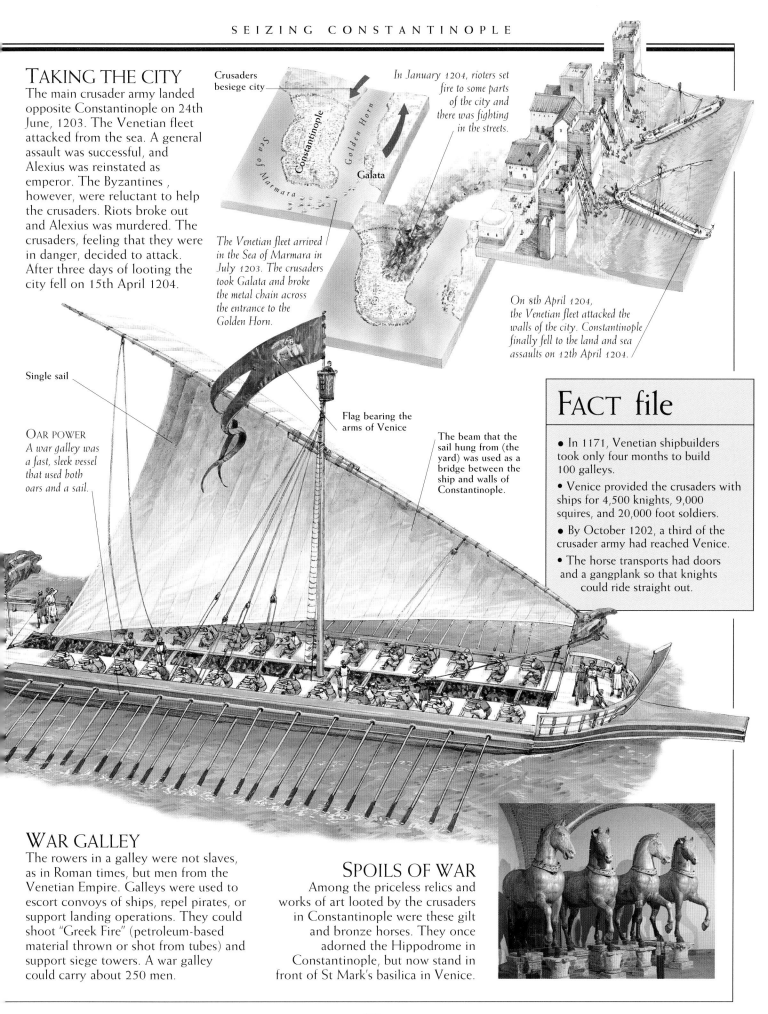

TAKING THE CITY

The main crusader army landed opposite Constantinople on 24th June, 1203. The Venetian fleet attacked from the sea. A general assault was successful, and Alexius was reinstated as emperor. The Byzantines, however, were reluctant to help the crusaders. Riots broke out and Alexius was murdered. The crusaders, feeling that they were in danger, decided to attack. After three days of looting the city fell on 15th April 1204.

Crusaders besiege city

In January 1204, rioters set fire to some parts of the city and there was fighting in the streets.

Sea of Marmara

Constantinople

Golden Horn

Galata

The Venetian fleet arrived in the Sea of Marmara in July 1203. The crusaders took Galata and broke the metal chain across the entrance to the Golden Horn.

On 8th April 1204, the Venetian fleet attacked the walls of the city. Constantinople finally fell to the land and sea assaults on 12th April 1204.

Single sail

OAR POWER
A war galley was a fast, sleek vessel that used both oars and a sail.

Flag bearing the arms of Venice

The beam that the sail hung from (the yard) was used as a bridge between the ship and walls of Constantinople.

FACT file

- In 1171, Venetian shipbuilders took only four months to build 100 galleys.
- Venice provided the crusaders with ships for 4,500 knights, 9,000 squires, and 20,000 foot soldiers.
- By October 1202, a third of the crusader army had reached Venice.
- The horse transports had doors and a gangplank so that knights could ride straight out.

WAR GALLEY

The rowers in a galley were not slaves, as in Roman times, but men from the Venetian Empire. Galleys were used to escort convoys of ships, repel pirates, or support landing operations. They could shoot "Greek Fire" (petroleum-based material thrown or shot from tubes) and support siege towers. A war galley could carry about 250 men.

SPOILS OF WAR

Among the priceless relics and works of art looted by the crusaders in Constantinople were these gilt and bronze horses. They once adorned the Hippodrome in Constantinople, but now stand in front of St Mark's basilica in Venice.

LATER CRUSADES

ORIGINALLY THE CRUSADES WERE Christian expeditions to recover the holy places, especially Jerusalem, from the Muslims. From the 12th century the word "crusade", which comes from French and Spanish for "cross", was used to describe any war urged by the Church for religious reasons. In 1213, the pope called for a fifth crusade to protect the crusader states in the Holy Land. The crusaders invaded Egypt, but failed to take it. For the next 200 years, there were many smaller "crusades", or holy wars, in various parts of the world. Most were against groups who seemed to threaten the Catholic Church.

A WORLD OF CRUSADES

Throughout this period, crusades were launched all over the known world. This tended to happen wherever a religious group felt threatened or others did not share their faith. The Teutonic Knights continued to try to bring Christianity to the people of the Baltic. Crusades were fought against the Cathars in southern France and the Hussites in Bohemia. The Spaniards pushed out the Moors from Spain in 1492, then tried to take their religion to Africa, England, and America.

THE HUSSITES
In the early 15th century Jan Huss was burned at the stake. His followers in Bohemia – the Hussites – revolted against the Germans who ruled there.

THE CATHARS
In the 13th century, Cathar heretics – Albigensians, – were crushed by French crusaders.

THE SPANISH CRUSADES
In the 16th century, the Spanish led crusades to North Africa to seize ports.

Catholic "crusaders"

IN THE 16TH CENTURY, Spanish conquistadors conquered the Aztecs and Maya in Central America, and the Incas in Peru. Their aim was to bring Christianity to these civilizations, but they were also in search of the legendary golden city of El Dorado.

Unknown creatures
The Aztecs, Maya, and Incas had not seen horses before and thought if the rider was killed, the horse was useless.

Conquistador

Inca warrior

THE SPANISH ARMADA
In 1588, Pope Sixtus V called for Spain to invade England, which was not Catholic, but Protestant. The Spanish fleet – the Armada – was attacked by English warships and broken up by fire-ships. On the way home the fleet was wrecked by fierce storms.

HUSSITE PROTEST

Persecuted by the Germans in Bohemia (now Slovakia) for breaking with the Catholic Church, the Hussites led a nationwide protest for religious freedom. They defended themselves from behind mobile "war wagons".

Horses were coralled within the wagon circle, safe from the Hussites' enemies.

From their wagons, the Hussites used cannon, hand guns, crossbows, and flails (spiked clubs on long handles).

PUSHING EAST
Teutonic Knights converted the Slavs to Christianity and settled in Prussia, Livonia, and Lithuania. They even pushed into Russia.

THE POPES' WARS
Various popes raised troops against their own enemies in the 12th and 13th centuries, especially the German emperors who invaded Italy.

INVASION OF THE BALKANS
From the 14th to 18th centuries, there were crusades to stop the Ottoman Turks advancing into the Balkans (Bulgaria, Greece, Hungary, and Serbia).

BALKANS

Constantinople

ANATOLIA (TURKEY)

CONSTANTINOPLE
The city of Constantinople never really recovered from the looting of 1204. In 1453, it fell to the Ottoman Turks.

Lepanto

SEA

BATTLE OF LEPANTO
In 1571, Venetians and Spaniards defeated an Ottoman fleet off Lepanto in Greece, stopping their movement west into the Mediterranean.

JANOS HUNYADI

Constantinople fell to the Ottoman Turks in 1453. A crusade was launched to drive out the Ottomans, who were trying to move into Hungary. In 1455 the Hungarian ruler, Janos Hunyadi, together with the preacher, John of Capistrano, defeated the huge Ottoman army. Both men died before they could drive the Ottoman Turks right out of Europe. The struggle with the Ottomans went on for over 200 years.

Guns – big and small

DURING THE 14TH CENTURY, guns began to be used. The Hussites made use of massed gunfire from behind their wagons to bring down armoured knights. The Ottoman, Sultan Mehmet, used huge cannon, called bombards, to blast the walls of Constantinople in 1453.

Handguns
By the late 14th century hand guns had been developed. The Hussites used them to good effect against the German crusaders.

The first hand guns were clumsy weapons. A shield helped to prop up the larger ones when taking aim.

Large shields called pavises were popular with those who used hand-guns. They provided some protection from flights of arrows.

SULTAN MEHMET
In the 14th century the Ottoman Turks began pushing into the Balkans. Crusades were called to defend Constantinople, which lay between the Ottomans and the Balkans. In 1453, the Ottoman Sultan, Mehmet II, besieged and captured the city, which is now called Istanbul.

FACT file

- In 1212, thousands of European children set off for the Holy Land on the Children's Crusade. Most of them died on the way or were captured and sold as slaves.

- In 1229, on the Fifth Crusade, German emperor, Frederick II, made a treaty with the Muslims. It gave control of Jerusalem back to the Christians.

- Crusades were called in 1236, when the Mongols from Asia invaded eastern Europe. Later, the Mongols left of their own accord.

WHAT CAME FROM THE CRUSADES?

THEY MAY HAVE SOURED RELATIONS between the Arab world and European Christians, yet some crusaders settled for a time in the Holy Land and learned to respect their Muslim neighbours. Contact with Muslim culture also brought aspects of Arab learning (especially mathematics, astronomy, and the arts) to Europe. Muslims had invaded Spain and Sicily and lived with Christians for years, so much Arab influence had already come from these areas. During and after the Crusades, silks and clothing, exotic foods, and new styles of decoration were increasingly seen in Europe. Even new words were found in European languages.

GIANT CATAPULT

This type of catapult – a trebuchet – worked like a see-saw. When the short end was pulled down, the longer end swung up and released its missile, such as a stone. Trebuchets first appeared in the Arab world in the 8th century and may have come to Europe with the crusaders. They do not seem to have been used in Europe until the 12th century.

MASSIVE LEVER
The longer end of the wooden arm swung up when the short end was pulled down.

TIMBER POWER
Catapults with huge counterweights could throw a missile the size of a horse.

ARAB INSTRUMENT

Tuning pegs

Fingerboard

Strings

The lute is a stringed instrument that was popular among Arabs, and came to Europe at the time of the Crusades. Early lutes were played with a plectrum – a small piece of ivory or quill for plucking the strings. From the 15th century, players used their fingers to pluck. The lute became an important instrument in the 16th century. It was the first instrument for which a large amount of music was written.

Sound box

PULLING POWER
A team of men pulled on the ropes to lower the beam. In later versions, a heavily weighted box did the job much better.

NAVIGATION SKILL

The Muslims studied the stars and understood astronomy. They used astrolabes (instruments that measured the distance of the stars from the Earth), to work out the position of ships at sea. Astrolabes were copied in Europe and used in ships' navigation.

Astrolabe

SLINGING IT
The missile sat in a rope sling that opened as it swung upwards.

Glasses

SUPERIOR SIGHT

Transparent quartz was used to make the first magnifying lenses. Recorded in Europe in the 13th century, they originally came from countries in the East, by way of the Arabs. By the 14th century, glasses like these were being made in a Venice factory. Glass mirrors were another Arab invention.

PIGEON POST

Using birds to carry messages was an Arabic idea, almost certainly brought to Europe from the Muslim world.

Knight   Foot soldier

A sad homecoming
Not everyone came home from the crusades triumphant. Many came back with no money or badly maimed (crippled). However Christians believed that going on a crusade made a place in heaven more likely.

Medicine

ARAB AND JEWISH MEDICINE was far more advanced than European medicine, though some medical schools in Constantinople used Greek and Roman teaching. An Arabic medical textbook called *al-Quanun* ("The Canon"), written in the early 11th century, was brought to Europe and used for hundreds of years.

Surgical skills

Muslim surgeons had many instruments for operations, and were shocked by the crudeness of crusader surgeons, especially those who simply cut off a leg with an axe. Muslim doctors used herbs and natural oils as medicines. Islamic teaching also stressed the importance of hygiene.

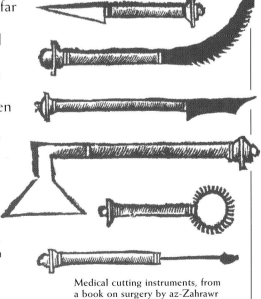
Medical cutting instruments, from a book on surgery by az-Zahrawr

FACT file

• Soap was an Arab import to Europe. Washing with soap reflected the importance of cleanliness for Muslims.

• Income tax began as a way of raising money for crusaders.

• The cruzada (a crusade tax linked to the Church) was not abolished in Pueblo, Colorado, USA, until 1945.

• In March 2000, Pope John Paul II apologized for Christian violence in the world, including the Crusades.

How do we know about THE CRUSADES?

W E KNOW A LOT ABOUT the crusades, but what are our sources? In other words, where do we get the evidence that helps us piece together the story? The skills of different experts can help. Historians who are able to read old languages translate books and documents. Architectural historians can tell how a building used to look from its ruins. Art historians can date pictures. All this information gives us an idea of what it was like at the time of the crusades.

I WAS NOT THERE

Some writers who did not take part in the crusades still felt they were able to write a good account. They got their information from returning pilgrims and soldiers or from other existing accounts. There were also poems and songs written about the crusades, sometimes to inspire recruits, sometimes for loved ones far away.

ALBERT OF AIX

WRITING HISTORY
Monks such as Albert of Aix often acted as clerks or scribes to record events. In the 12th century, Aix in the south of France was a religious centre.

Albert of Aix
In about 1130, Albert wrote the fullest history of the First Crusade. It blends facts and legends, and these would need to be disentangled to reach a true account of events.

***Historia Rerum in Partibus Transmarinis Gestarum* (1169-87), by William of Tyre.**
The greatest crusader historian, William of Tyre wrote 70 years after the First Crusade. He covered the period 1095–1184. He used the work of Albert of Aix to recount the events of the First Crusade, but then added records and traditions that survived in the crusader lands. He tried to understand the causes of the crusades and what happened during them.

Kamil at-Tawarikh **(A History), by Ibn Al-Athir of Mosul**
Ibn al-Athir was the greatest Muslim historian of the 13th century. His early writings are brief, but for the late 12th–century material he used writers in Saladin's army. For the middle period (c. 1150) he used original accounts and tried to understand the causes of the crusades.

WELL-DRESSED KNIGHT
From accounts and pictures of the time, historians can tell what a crusader knight would have worn. This knight of about 1250 wears a shirt of mail with a cloth surcoat over the top. He has a helmet, and carries a shield and lance.

A 13TH-CENTURY KNIGHT

I WAS THERE

Sometimes we are lucky enough to have eyewitness accounts by people who went on the crusades or met crusaders. As well as first-hand accounts, diaries and letters also survive.

Life of Alexius Comnenus by Anna Comnena
The Byzantine emperor, Alexius I, had a daughter named Anna. She witnessed the arrival of the leaders and soldiers of the First Crusade in Constantinople and wrote about it, around 1140. Anna's words show how wary the Byzantines were of strangers. She described one of the crusader leaders, Bohemond, and how treacherous she felt him to be.

EMPEROR ALEXIUS I COMNENUS

***Gesta Francorum* (Deeds of the Franks)**
An account from the First Crusade. It conveys the feelings of an ordinary soldier, who went into battle.

Life of Saladin, by Beha ed-Din
The writer was one of Saladin's attendants. He based his book mainly on hearsay (rumours), although it contains some of Saladin's own thoughts. Beha ed-Din probably wrote after Saladin's death in 1193.

Letters by Stephen, Count of Blois
Stephen wrote to his wife, William the Conqueror's daughter, from the First Crusade. One letter came from the camp before Nicaea (1097), another from just before Antioch (1098).

A MIXTURE OF SOURCES

Some sources began as eyewitness accounts but have only reached us in versions rewritten by other people, who were not actually present on the crusades.

***Itinerarium Ricardi* (King Richard's Journey, c. 1200)**
Apparently written by an Englishman, this account is more like a story. The writer describes the exploits of Richard the Lionheart during the Third Crusade.

***Estoire de la Guerre Sainte* (History of the Holy War, c. 1200)**
Similar to "King Richard's Journey", but written in French. Both works may have been taken from the same account, written by a soldier in Richard's army.

BUILDINGS TELL A STORY

Perhaps the most obvious sources of information about the crusades are the huge castles and fortifications built by the crusaders and the Muslims. One of these castles is Krak des Chevaliers in Syria. Other buildings include churches, such as the Holy Sepulchre in Jerusalem, and the merchant quarters (areas) in Acre.

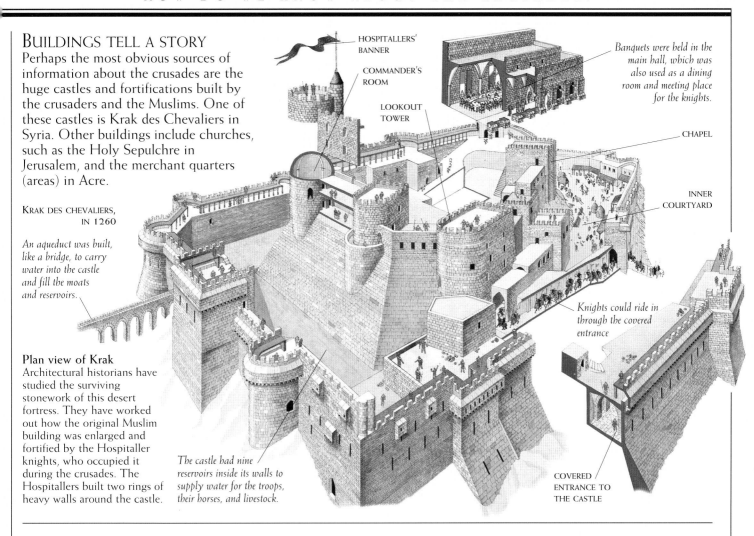

KRAK DES CHEVALIERS, IN 1260

An aqueduct was built, like a bridge, to carry water into the castle and fill the moats and reservoirs.

HOSPITALLERS' BANNER

COMMANDER'S ROOM

LOOKOUT TOWER

Banquets were held in the main hall, which was also used as a dining room and meeting place for the knights.

CHAPEL

INNER COURTYARD

Knights could ride in through the covered entrance

Plan view of Krak
Architectural historians have studied the surviving stonework of this desert fortress. They have worked out how the original Muslim building was enlarged and fortified by the Hospitaller knights, who occupied it during the crusades. The Hospitallers built two rings of heavy walls around the castle.

The castle had nine reservoirs inside its walls to supply water for the troops, their horses, and livestock.

COVERED ENTRANCE TO THE CASTLE

OFFICIAL RECORDS

Surviving official documents provide hard facts. A copy of Pope Innocent III's proclamation for the Fifth Crusade gives a good idea of how he encouraged people to join the crusades. Financial records show how expensive the crusades were, and how people were taxed to help fund them. For example, in England, the "Saladin Tithe" of 1188 demanded that each person should pay a tenth of their income or livestock.

History from art
The information that we get from illuminated manuscript pictures, engravings, and coins is invaluable. Some of these works of art show how various cultures influenced one another. However, pictures must be assessed by an expert – in many cases the illustrations in a chronicle (register of events) may have been made hundreds of years after the event, when costumes and armour had changed.

A 12TH-CENTURY SEAL, SHOWING TWO TEMPLAR KNIGHTS ON ONE HORSE SYMBOLISING THEIR VOW OF POVERTY.

Objects as evidence
Many crusader objects have survived, including sculpture, pottery, and even glass beakers. They allow us to see what people would have used and worn at the time. They also tell us about the different methods used by different cultures to make the objects.

CRUSADER POTTERY
A piece of a pottery jar found lying outside the town of Caesarea is evidence of an everyday item made and used by the crusaders.

POTTERY SHARD FROM CAESAREA

Being there

READING ABOUT THE crusades is exciting, but nothing beats actually seeing some of the historic places. How ever much they have changed, it still gives a feeling of the size of places – cities, buildings, castles, or battlefields – and helps you imagine the events that took place there.

A mosque to visit
The al-Aqsa mosque in Jerusalem was built on the site of King Solomon's temple. The order of Knights Templars was founded here in 1118 during the crusades.

AL-AQSA MOSQUE

CRUSADES AT A GLANCE

THE ENTRIES BELOW SHOW the main events of the crusades, including major crusades, and some less important expeditions to the Holy Land. Later crusades, to other parts of the world, are also listed.

THE CAPTURE OF JERUSALEM

AD 330
Emperor Constantine established Byzantium as "New Rome" in the east.

AD 622
The Muslim calendar began this year.

1071
The Seljuk Turks seized Asia Minor. The Byzantines were defeated by the Seljuks at the Battle of Manzikert.

1095
The Byzantines appealed to the Pope in Rome for help against the Seljuks. The result was Pope Urban II's journey through France, urging people to join the First Crusade.

1096
The First Crusade left for the Holy Land. Peter the Hermit's crusade was defeated in Anatolia.

1097
The surrender of Nicaea to the Byzantines. The crusaders won a victory over the Seljuks at the Battle of Dorylaeum. The siege of Antioch began.

BATTLE OF DORYLAEUM

1098
The first crusader state, the County of Edessa, was established by Baldwin of Flanders. The Muslims were defeated at the Battle of Antioch outside the city.

1099
The crusaders captured the holy city of Jerusalem. The French crusader, Godfrey of Bouillon, was elected ruler of Jerusalem. The Egyptians were defeated at the Battle of Ascalon.

1107
Sigurd of Norway's expedition to the Holy Land was more like a pilgrimage. The crusade of Bohemond of Taranto lasted one year.

1118
The Templars were founded in Jerusalem, with headquarters at al-Aqsa mosque.

TEMPLAR KNIGHT

1122-26
A crusade was proclaimed by Pope Calixtus II. Tyre in the Holy Land was captured by crusaders in 1124 and Malaga in Spain in 1125.

1128
A new crusade was preached by, among others, Hugh of Payns, Grand Master of the Order of Knights Templars.

1129
The crusaders attacked the town of Damascus.

1131-52
Melisande reigned as queen of Jerusalem.

1144
Zengi captured Edessa on Christmas Eve while Joscelin II, Count of Edessa, was away.

1146
Jews in the Rhineland (now Germany) were persecuted. St Bernard preached the Second Crusade, which was led by Louis VII of France and Conrad III of Germany.

1147
The Second Crusade extended to Spain, where King Alphonso VII of Castile captured Almeria. The Crusade was taken up by leaders in Saxony, who attacked the non-religious Wends (Slavic people) in the Baltic.

1148
Louis VII of France went to Jerusalem rather than Edessa. The crusaders, together with King Baldwin III of Jerusalem, attacked Damascus but were not able to take it.

1158-75
Spanish orders of knights were founded, the first one being the Order of Calatrava. A crusade was authorized in Spain.

1187
Saladin captured King Guy of Jerusalem at the Battle of Hattin and took the crusaders' relic, the True Cross. A Third Crusade was called.

THE BATTLE OF HATTIN

1190
German Emperor Frederick I drowned in the River Calycadnus in Anatolia. His crusading army fell apart.

1191
Philip II of France landed at Acre. Richard I of England took the island of Cyprus before arriving in the Holy Land. The crusaders captured Acre. Saladin's army were driven back at the Battle of Arsuf.

1192
Richard came close to Jerusalem, but knew he could not take it, so he made a treaty with Saladin. He was shipwrecked and captured on his return to England.

1195
Muslim victory at Alarcos in Spain.

1197-98
Emperor Henry VI organised the German Crusade, which helped win back Sidon and Beirut in the Holy Land. The campaign collapsed when the Germans heard of the death of their emperor back home.

1198
The Fourth Crusade was proclaimed by Pope Innocent III.

CRUSADES IN THE HOLY LAND

On the timeline (right) the figures represent the major crusades to the Holy Land, from the 11th century until the fall of the crusader states in 1291. After the Fifth Crusade, the expeditions are not usually numbered, although many were large. From the late 11th century to the late 13th century, crusaders set out to defend Christianity against what they saw as the Muslim threat.

CAPTURE OF JERUSALEM	
1096 1099	1146
FIRST CRUSADE STARTS	SECOND CRUSADE STARTS

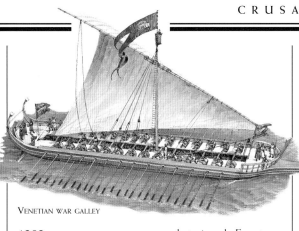
VENETIAN WAR GALLEY

1202
The Fourth Crusade sailed for the Holy Land with financial help from the Doge of Venice. The crusaders captured the town of Zara.

1203-4
Crusaders landed at Chalcedon and captured Galata in Anatolia (Turkey). Alexius III fled. Byzantine hostility to the crusaders resulted in the raid on Contantinople.

1209-29
Pope Innocent III's crusade against Cathar heretics (Albigensians) in southern France.

1212
The Children's Crusade set out from Germany, reached Genoa in Italy and marched to Rome, where it fell apart. Pope Innocent III called for a new Spanish crusade and the crusaders won a victory at Las Navas de Tolosa in central Spain.

1213
Pope Innocent III proclaimed a Fifth Crusade, to win back Jerusalem, but he died the following year and nothing was done.

1217
Crusaders arrived in the Holy Land, led by Duke Leopold of Austria, King Andrew of Hungary, and King Hugh I of Cyprus.

1218
King Andrew left for home. The decision was made to invade Egypt. The Fifth Crusade landed near Damietta in Egypt and captured the town the following year.

1221
The crusaders were joined by Duke Louis of Bavaria. They reached Mansurah in Egypt, but were cut off and forced to leave the country.

1229
Emperor Frederick II agreed a treaty with the Egyptians that gave control of Jerusalem, as well as parts of the Holy Land, to the Christians. Frederick ruled Jerusalem until 1243.

1236-42
Fierce invaders from Mongolia (the Mongols) invaded Russia and eastern Europe under their leader Batu Khan. Crusades were preached by Popes Gregory IX and Innocent V. The Mongols withdrew.

MONGOL WARRIORS

1239-41
Crusade led by French Count Thibald of Champagne and English Earl Richard of Cornwall. Despite Thibald's defeat by the Egyptians at Gaza, a treaty gave the kingdom of Jerusalem more land than at any time since 1187.

1242
Russian Prince Alexander Nevsky defeated the invading Teutonic Knights on the frozen Lake Peipus in Russia.

1248-49
The crusade of King Louis IX of France reached Cyprus, then moved to Egypt the following May. Damietta fell to the crusaders.

1250
Crusaders launched an attack on Mansurah, which was defeated. The crusader army retreated and Louis surrendered.

1265-68
The Mamluks (soldier-slaves in Egypt) captured the crusader towns of Caesarea, Arsur, Saphet, and Antioch.

1270
Crusade of Louis IX of France to Tunis in North Africa. Disease killed Louis, so a treaty was made and the crusader army sailed to Sicily.

1291
Acre fell to the Mamluks under Sultan al-Ashraf Khalil. The Christians left the Holy Land.

1306-9
From their base in Cyprus, the Knights Hospitallers invaded Rhodes in Greece and based themselves there.

1312
The Knights Templars were banned by Philip IV of France, who envied their wealth.

1365
King Peter I of Cyprus led a crusade to Egypt and captured Alexandria.

1383
The Bishop of Norwich in England, a supporter of the pope in Rome, led a crusade against the Count of Flanders, who backed another pope at Avignon in France. This was at a time when there were two popes in office.

1396
A Hungarian and French crusade against the Ottomans in the Balkans was backed by the popes in Rome and Avignon. The crusaders were beaten by the Ottomans at Nicopolis in Bulgaria.

1410
Teutonic Knights were defeated by Christian Poles and Lithuanians at Tannenberg in Poland.

TEUTONIC KNIGHT

1453
Constantinople fell to the Ottoman Turks led by Sultan Mehmet.

1492
Granada, the last Moorish city in Spain, fell to Spanish troops.

1497-1578
The Spanish and Portuguese seized towns in North Africa. King Sebastian of Portugal was killed at Alcazarquivir in Morocco in 1578.

1519
The Spaniard Hernan Cortés was sent to Mexico. In two years he conquered the Aztecs.

1522
The Ottomans besieged Rhodes and the Hospitallers were forced to surrender. They left the following year.

1530
The Hospitallers were given Malta, and Tripoli in North Africa, by Emperor Charles V.

1532
Francisco Pizarro from Spain conquered the Inca Empire in Peru.

1551
Tripoli surrendered to the Ottomans.

1565
The Hospitallers defended Malta against the Ottomans.

1571
A fleet of ships under Don John of Austria defeated the Ottoman navy at the Battle of Lepanto, off southern Greece. The western Mediterranean was now safe from the Turks.

1588
Spain sent warships – the Armada – against England. The fleet was beaten by bad weather.

THE ARMADA

1683
The Ottomans besieged Vienna in Austria. They were driven out by a crusading army of mainly Polish soldiers. Land in the Balkans was regained for the Christians.

1798
The Hospitallers surrendered to Emperor Napoleon I in Malta.

BATTLE OF HATTIN/THIRD CRUSADE

SECOND CRUSADE OF ST LOUIS

1187 1198 FOURTH CRUSADE STARTS 1221 FIFTH CRUSADE STARTS 1248 FIRST CRUSADE OF ST LOUIS 1270 SECOND CRUSADE OF ST LOUIS 1291 CRUSADERS LEAVE THE HOLY LAND

Index

Acknowledgments

The publisher would like to thank:
Terry Jones for his help with this book, Sheila Collins for design help and Chris Bernstein for providing the index.

The publisher would like to thank the following for their kind permission to reproduce their photographs:

a=above; c=centre; b=below; l=left; r=right; t=top.

Ancient Art & Architecture Collection: 45bl; Chris Hellier 10bl; R Sheridan 39br, 43cl. The Art Archive: Bibliotheque de l'Arsenal, Paris 16clb; Haghia Sofia, Istanbul 11tc; Musee du Louvre 12tr; Uffizi Gallery, Florence. Bridgeman Art Library, London / New York: Bibliotheque Nationale Paris, France 17tr; 37crb; 24–25, 32–33; 14tl, 14b, 15tl; British Library, London 30cl; 37cra; Estoire d' Outremer 20cl; Landes Bibliothek, Filda 36clb; Musee Conde, Chantilly, France / Tres Riches Heures de Duc de Berry (early 15th Century) 6tl, 6tr, 6b; San Marco, Venice 9tl;

V & A Museum 8tl. Corbis UK Ltd: Oriol Alamany & E Vicens 19cr. Board of Trustees of the Armories, Tower of London: 44cr. Sonia Halliday Photographs: 12tl, 13tl, 41cr. Robert Harding Picture Library: Bildagentur Schuster/Meir 289t; K. Gillham 13tr; P. Hawkins 27crb. © Michael Holford: 26tl. N.H.P.A.: Manfred Danegger 27crb. Public Record Office Picture Library: 36tl. Zev Radovan, Jerusalem: 45br. Tony Smith/Virail Pomfres: 12–13. Art Directors & TRIP: B Turner 29c; Jeff Greenberg 28crb. The Wallace Collection: 26cr, 26–27, 27clb.

Jacket:

The Art Archive: Musee de Louvre back inside flap. Bridgeman Art Library, London / New York: Bibliotheque de Municipale front tl; Bibliotheque Nationale, Paris, France back br. Robert Harding Picture Library: front c. Wallace Collection: front bfl, front bl.